PRO WRESTLING'S GREATEST
FACES

BY MATT SCHEFF

SportsZone

An Imprint of Abdo Publishing
abdopublishing.com

abdopublishing.com

Published by Abdo Publishing, a division of ABDO, PO Box 398166, Minneapolis, Minnesota 55439. Copyright © 2017 by Abdo Consulting Group, Inc. International copyrights reserved in all countries. No part of this book may be reproduced in any form without written permission from the publisher. SportsZone™ is a trademark and logo of Abdo Publishing.

Printed in the United States of America, North Mankato, Minnesota
102016
012017

Cover Photo: Jonathan Bachman/WWE/AP Images
Interior Photos: Jonathan Bachman/WWE/AP Images, 1; Matt Roberts/ZumaPress/Icon Sportswire, 4; Rick Scuteri/AP Images, 5; Helga Esteb/Shutterstock Images, 6-7, 8; Mark Serota/ WWE/AP Images, 9; Guillermo Granados/Notimex/Newscom, 10-11; Yukio Hiraku/AFLO/ Newscom, 12; Marty Lederhandler/AP Images, 13; Revelli-Beaumont/SIPA/Newscom, 14-15; Leon Halip/WireImage/Getty Images, 16-17; Bruce Bennett/Getty Images, 18-19; Don Feria/WWE/AP Images, 20-21; Bettmann/Getty Images, 22; Picture Perfect/Rex Features/AP Images, 23; Moses Robinson/Getty Images Entertainment/Getty Images, 24-25; Ann Clifford/DMI/The LIFE Picture Collection/Getty Images, 26; Russell Turiak/Hulton Archive/Getty Images, 27; George Pimentel/ WireImage/Getty Images, 28-29

Editor: Patrick Donnelly
Series Designer: Laura Polzin

Publisher's Cataloging-in-Publication Data
Names: Scheff, Matt, author.
Title: Pro wrestling's greatest faces / by Matt Scheff.
Description: Minneapolis, MN : Abdo Publishing, 2017. | Series: Pro wrestling's
    greatest | Includes bibliographical references and index.
Identifiers: LCCN 2016945678 | ISBN 9781680784947 (lib. bdg.) |
    ISBN 9781680798227 (ebook)
Subjects: LCSH: Wrestling--Juvenile literature. | Wrestlers--Juvenile literature.
Classification: DDC 796.812--dc23
LC record available at http://lccn.loc.gov/2016945678

TABLE OF CONTENTS

INTRODUCTION: SHOCKING TURN

One of the biggest matches at WrestleMania 13 in 1997 featured Bret Hart battling "Stone Cold" Steve Austin. Hart was a beloved babyface—a good guy. Austin was a heel. Hart's fans rained boos down on Austin. It was a brutal, bloody match. The wrestlers brawled inside the ring and out into the stands. Neither man would submit. But in time, Austin passed out. Much to the crowd's delight, Hart won the match.

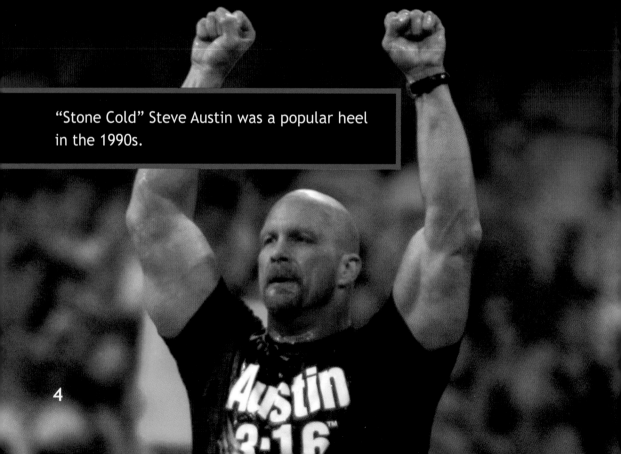

"Stone Cold" Steve Austin was a popular heel in the 1990s.

Bret Hart made a
memorable heel
turn in 1997.

Austin's newfound popularity led him to a career acting in movies.

But the brutality didn't stop there. Hart continued to attack the unconscious Austin. The cheers for him turned into boos. As the referee finally pulled Hart away, everything had changed. Hart was no longer a face. His actions had turned him into a heel. And Austin came away with a new image as a face. It was a rare and unforgettable double turn that changed the landscape of World Wrestling Entertainment (WWE) for years to come.

TEN

THE ROCK

Dwayne Johnson burst onto the WWE scene in 1996. He was known as Rocky Maivia at the time, but he soon changed his ring name to The Rock. Many fans know The Rock as a heel. But "The People's Champion" spent much of his early career as the most popular face in WWE. In the 2000s, he turned his talents to Hollywood. Johnson starred in movies such as *The Scorpion King*, *Race to Witch Mountain*, and *San Andreas*.

These days Dwayne Johnson is known more for his acting career than his wrestling days.

The Rock was both a face and a heel during his career.

NINE

REY MYSTERIO

Many fans call Rey Mysterio the greatest high-flyer in pro wrestling history. Mysterio stands just 5 feet 6 inches (168 cm) tall. He weighs only 175 pounds (79 kg). Yet he goes toe-to-toe with men much larger than himself, and the fans love him for it.

A FAMILY AFFAIR

Many pro wrestlers, including The Rock and Rey Mysterio, have wrestling in their families. Mysterio learned to wrestle from his uncle. The Rock's father and grandfather were both pro wrestlers.

Rey Mysterio delivers a high-flying kick to a hapless foe.

They didn't come much bigger than Andre the Giant.

EIGHT

ANDRE THE GIANT

Andre the Giant lived up to his name. Standing 7 feet 4 inches (224 cm) tall and weighing more than 500 pounds (227 kg), he was a mountain of a man. And his personality was just as big. He won over fans with his kind nature and hard work in the ring. Andre made a heel turn late in his career, feuding with the popular Hulk Hogan. But most fans remember him as a beloved face.

Andre the Giant compares fists with heavyweight boxer Chuck Wepner in 1976.

Kofi Kingston flies high to take down Santino Marella in 2008.

SEVEN

KOFI KINGSTON

Kofi Kingston's big smile and raw athletic style made him a hit with fans the moment he joined WWE in 2008. Kingston thrives in singles and tag-team matches. He has won multiple singles titles and been part of many championship tag teams. He excites fans with his signature moves, including the flying Boom Drop.

SIX

"STONE COLD" STEVE AUSTIN

"Stone Cold" Steve Austin would become one of WWE's all-time heels. But first he was a face. In the late 1990s, he helped launch WWE's popular Attitude Era, and he redefined what a face could be. He ignored the classic "good guy" routine, and the fans loved him anyway. Injuries forced Austin to retire in 2003.

BLURRED LINES

For decades the roles of babyface and heel were clear. Faces were good. Heels were bad. But that line started to blur in the late 1990s. Fans began cheering for heels and booing babyfaces. Most modern wrestlers now combine traits of both.

"Stone Cold" Steve Austin was so popular he sometimes served as a celebrity referee.

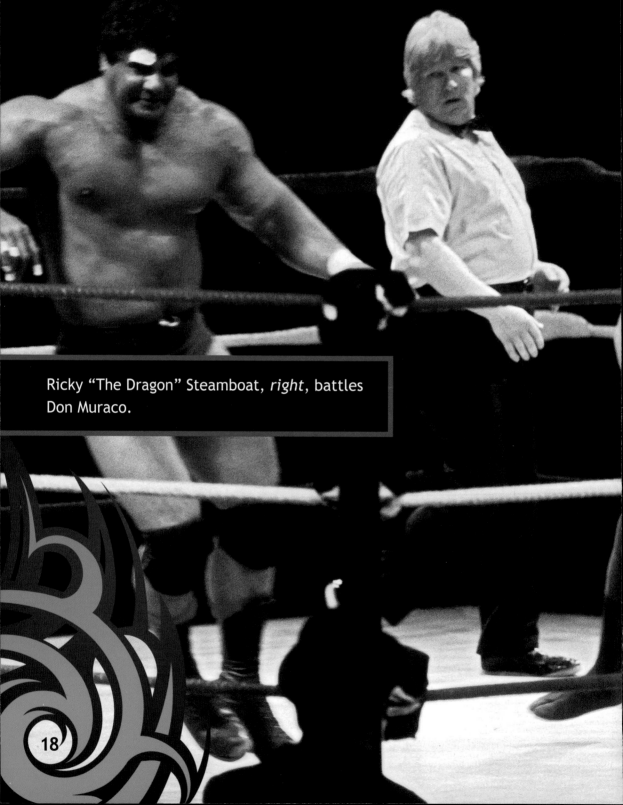

Ricky "The Dragon" Steamboat, *right*, battles Don Muraco.

FIVE

RICKY "THE DRAGON" STEAMBOAT

Ricky "The Dragon" Steamboat was a classic 1980s face. The Hawaii native was a clean-cut family man who fought fair. He starred in singles wrestling and was a tag-team specialist. Fans loved his long rivalry with heel Ric Flair. Their matches, including an epic at the Chi-Town Rumble in 1989, have become legendary.

FOUR

STING

In the late 1980s, Sting was the biggest star of World Championship Wrestling (WCW). The ex-bodybuilder thrived in the ring and on the microphone. *Pro Wrestling Illustrated* named him Most Popular Wrestler of the Year a record four times. Sting made his name as a face, but he turned heel late in his career. He retired in 2016 at age 56.

Sting appeared at WrestleMania 31 in 2015.

THREE

BRUNO SAMMARTINO

Italian-born Bruno Sammartino was one of the earliest pro wrestling stars. Sammartino was big and strong. He overpowered opponents. In 1963 he won the WWE title after pinning Buddy Rogers in just 48 seconds. His legend only grew from there. Sammartino held the WWE championship for a combined 11 years.

Sammartino has the upper hand on The Sheik in this match at Madison Square Garden in New York.

Bruno Sammartino, *top*, brings the pain to Sgt. Slaughter.

WWE HALL OF FAME

The greatest legends in pro wrestling are honored in the WWE Hall of Fame. That includes singles wrestlers, tag teams, and other groups. More than 100 wrestlers have been honored so far.

John Cena is declared the winner of a match in 2011.

TWO

JOHN CENA

John Cena is the face of modern pro wrestling. Fans love him both inside the ring and out. The wrestler, actor, and musician has won more than 20 championship belts. He's also set another record. Cena has granted more wishes in the Make-A-Wish program than anyone in history. It's no wonder fans roar every time he steps into the ring.

ONE

HULK HOGAN

The biggest star in pro wrestling history is Hulk Hogan. In the 1980s, Hogan's popularity in the ring was unmatched. And "Hulkamania" didn't stop there. Hogan became a full-blown pop culture star. Even people who didn't care about pro wrestling declared themselves "Hulkamaniacs." Hogan was on TV, in advertisements, and in movies.

Hogan, pictured with Mr. T and Cyndi Lauper, was a huge celebrity in the 1980s.

Hulk Hogan raises a championship belt.

In 1987 Hogan thrilled fans at WrestleMania 3 when he battled Andre the Giant. Hogan lifted the giant and slammed him to the mat. Hogan built his popularity as the greatest face in WWE history. That's why his 1996 heel turn in WCW shocked everyone. "Hollywood" Hulk Hogan went on to become one of pro wrestling's all-time great heels.

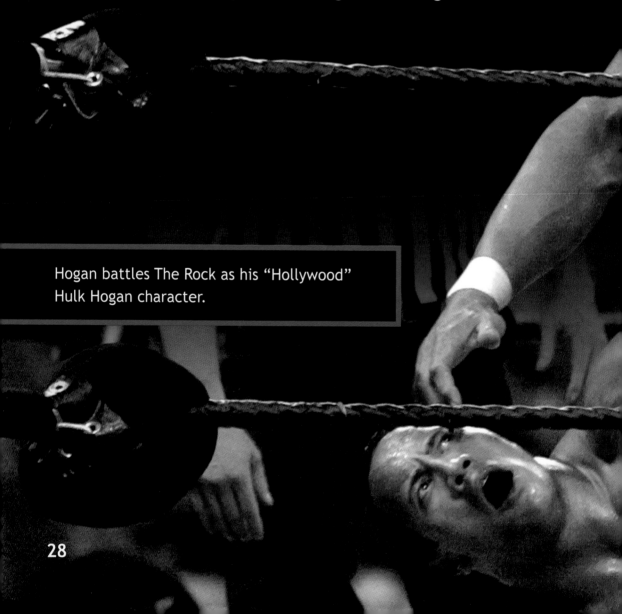

Hogan battles The Rock as his "Hollywood" Hulk Hogan character.

GLOSSARY

ATTITUDE ERA

A period in pro wrestling during the late 1990s and early 2000s, when pro wrestling marketed itself more strongly to adults.

BABYFACE

A wrestler seen as a good guy; also called a face.

DOUBLE TURN

An event that turns a babyface into a heel, and at the same time, a heel into a babyface.

FEUD

A bitter disagreement between two or more people.

HEEL

A wrestler seen as a villain.

HEEL TURN

The event that marks the changing of a good guy (babyface) into a villain (heel).

RIVALRY

A long-standing, intense, and often emotional competition between two people or teams.

SIGNATURE MOVE

A move for which a wrestler is best known.

FOR MORE INFORMATION

BOOKS

Kortemeier, Todd. *Superstars of WWE*. Mankato, MN: Amicus High Interest, 2016.

Scheff, Matt. *Pro Wrestling's Greatest Rivalries*. Minneapolis, MN: Abdo Publishing, 2017.

WEBSITES

To learn more about pro wrestling, visit booklinks.abdopublishing.com. These links are routinely monitored and updated to provide the most current information available.

INDEX

ABOUT THE AUTHOR

Matt Scheff is an artist and author living in Alaska. He enjoys mountain climbing, deep-sea fishing, and curling up with his two Siberian huskies to watch wrestling.